A PRACTICAL GUIDE FOR

SELF CHANGE

A PRACTICAL GUIDE FOR

SELF CHANGE

Diana Hutchison

Illustrations by Rod Hutchison

Copyright © 2022, by Diana Hutchison. All rights reserved. No part of this publication may be reproduced or transmitted in any form by any means, electronic or mechanical, including photocopying, recording or by any information storage and retrieval system, without permission in writing to the publisher. For information contact the publisher/author:

First Edition 2022

Author: Diana Hutchison
Title: A Practical Guide For Self Change
ISBN: 978-0-6454262-0-5 paperback print
        978-0-6454262-1-2 ebook

A catalogue record for this book is available from the National Library of Australia

The publisher and author shall have neither liability nor responsibility to any person or entity with respect to any loss of damage caused, or alleged to have been caused, directly or indirectly by the information contained in this book. Inquiries should be made to the publisher/author:

Cover design: NGirl Design
Illustrations: Rod Hutchison

This book is for my mother Elizabeth, who loved and supported me, and who taught me the value of being there for others.

ACKNOWLEDGEMENTS

This book was conceived and written on the land of the Kaurna People.

We acknowledge and respect their spiritual relationship with their land and country. We also acknowledge the Kaurna people as the custodians of the Adelaide region and that their cultural and heritage beliefs are important through all time.

We acknowledge and pay our respects to the cultural authority of past, present and emerging leaders and acknowledge and listen to their voices and messages for greater cultural inclusion.

CONTENTS

Preface		1
Chapter 1	Starting Points for Change	5
Chapter 2	Taking Responsibility	17
Chapter 3	Observing Yourself	25
Chapter 4	Sorting out Values	41
Chapter 5	Sorting out Core Beliefs	55
Chapter 6	Discovering Issues	83
Chapter 7	Setting Goals	97
Chapter 8	Continuing the Process—Dealing with Negative Thoughts and Emotions	113
Chapter 9	Continuing the Process—Troubleshooting	129
Conclusion		143
References		145
About The Author		151

FREE DOWNLOADS

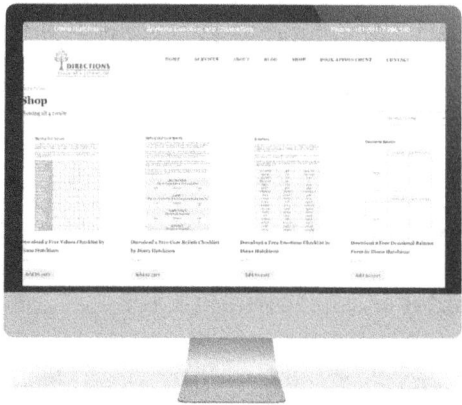

Grab your free downloads for self-assessment to accompany this book by visiting

www.dianahutchison.com/shop

PREFACE

This book has grown out of my own journey of self-discovery, as well as my experiences while I was a psychologist counselling many people through a range of issues over fifteen years. It draws on a number of texts that were part of my reading and have stood the test of time. It also has a basis in my study and experience of life coaching, especially in teaching goal setting.

I have written A Practical Guide for Self Change for people who are just starting out on their journey of self-discovery, or have started and now want to change themselves or their lives in some way. It combines explanations of the process of change with practical approaches to making changes.

Chapter 1 introduces the process of self-change, while chapters 2–6 cover responsibility, self-monitoring, values, beliefs and discovering issues, and serve as a preparation for developing goals to achieve change. Chapter 7 shows how to set achievable goals and chapters 8 and 9 offer ways of dealing with problems you may come up against in working on your goals. Full details of the texts I have referenced are at the end of the book.

To get the most out of A Practical Guide for Self Change, read the chapters consecutively and once you have finished the whole book, go back and do the suggested exercises.

If you are a survivor of child sexual assault or other traumatic events, it is recommended that you seek specialist help to assist you through your recovery and change process.

A Practical Guide for Self Change is intended as a simple introduction to self-change and I hope I have made it easy to understand.

I would like to thank the people who took the time to read my rough drafts and make comments, which I have incorporated into the book. In particular, I would like to thank my sister Mary Hutchison for her time and effort in editing.

CHAPTER 1
STARTING POINTS FOR CHANGE

Change? Why do it? It is your choice. You can remain where you are in your life with the problems that you have, or you can choose to think about what would happen if you did manage to change something in your life, even if it is only a very small change. Is there anything you would like to change?

This chapter provides you with the starting points for addressing change and helps you get ready for the process you are about to embark on.

DECIDING TO CHANGE

You change for you. Because you want something to be different. Not because others think you should. Any change that is desired has to be desired by you most of all.

Deciding to change your behaviour is a very important decision. And only you can do it. Only you can say, "That's it! I've had enough."

When we first say this to ourselves, we may think, and even believe, that what has to change is how others are behaving. This would naturally change how we behave, wouldn't it? It might seem so, but it depends on where the problem is. Is the problem in us or in others? Perhaps the problem is not so much another person's behaviour, but our interpretation and response to it.

While it may seem that the problem is in someone else's behaviour, we are not in control of other people and how they think and behave. We might be able to influence what they do, but essentially, we are only in control of ourselves and everything that goes with that.

We are in control of our behaviour, our emotions and thoughts, and we can choose to control these directly. And isn't it so much better to have that control? If you want to start changing something, no one is going to do it better or faster than you.

Once you start behaving differently, then others around you may also start to change, especially those you are very close to, like your loved ones, your friends, and workmates. This is because you are interacting with them and when you speak or act differently, they may respond to you differently. But this is not the reason for you to make changes. Any changes that others make are a by-product of your decision and action, and if those you wish would change don't, it is not your fault or your responsibility.

WHAT TO CHANGE

What would you like to change? This is an important question and a good starting point. Be realistic in your appraisal. There are some things that you can't change, like whether you are naturally an introvert or an extrovert, but you can change your feelings of ease in social situations, for example.

As an exercise in thinking about what to change, make a list of the characteristics that you like about yourself, including physical aspects, on one side of the page. With this however, it is not about outward appearance, but more about the inner feeling. For example, strength. On the other side of the page, make a list of the negative characteristics that you feel you would like to address. Again, be realistic and focus on what you can change. For instance, you could work on becoming more assertive, or not reacting angrily to certain situations.

Another way of thinking about what to change is to look at how you are operating in relation to your past, present and future. Your body is in the present, but you can be emotionally and mentally in the past, the present or the future. Are you in the present most of the time?

If you seem to spend a lot more time in the past or the future than you do in the present, it may indicate that you need to work on this in your change process. For instance, if you find that you think a lot about the past—whether a long time ago or only an hour ago—ask yourself what it is that is keeping you there. Is there some trauma, problem or worry that is blocking you from being in the present? If so, you may need to work on ways of letting the problem go.

On the other hand, if you find that you spend a lot of time worrying about the future, or just thinking about it without doing anything constructive, then perhaps you could think about taking some action now in order to construct a better future for yourself. "What ifs" are all very well, but they do not help you to become anybody or anything. Setting goals and working towards them through taking action in the present is going to be far more effective in creating a better future (see chapter 7 for setting goals).

It can be scary to think about changing. You may feel that if you are no longer acting in one way, you won't know what to do. Relax. You are still going to be you, even if you end up behaving a bit differently. It is not going to change who you are deep down.

Remember that you are much more than your thoughts. You are much more than your behaviour. You are much more than your emotions. You are much more than your beliefs. The whole you is much greater than the sum of all the parts.

UNDERSTANDING HOW CHANGE HAPPENS

You are not suddenly, all at once, going to be different. It is a gradual process and you may only realise that change has occurred when you look back. In hindsight, anyone can have 20/20 vision.

If you decide to make changes in your life, all you are really asking of yourself is to put into place, little by little, the things that you want to do differently. What is important is to break down the aspects of the desired behaviours, so that you can take small but realistic steps towards your goal.

Let's say, for instance, that you want to become more assertive. If you do some research and find examples of how to assert yourself in various situations, you will find that one of the obvious things that non-assertive people need to do more of is to say "No". The first step, therefore, is to start saying "No". When you do this, you will realise that the sky is not going to fall in just because you are paying attention to your own needs. Others will actually respect you for it.

In this example, learning to say "No" could be the first step on your road to change. You could set a goal around this, as described in chapter 7. When you are comfortable saying "No" in a variety of situations, then you can think about addressing another aspect of yourself that you would like to change—working out how to ask someone to change his or her behaviour, for instance.

In taking steps like these, you are gradually making little changes in the now, the present, as you are going along in your daily life. Each little change in the present moment adds up to great change over a longer time and small steps make the process less scary.

RECOGNISING THE PROBLEM

In order to change we need to be able to recognise our problems. This means that we need to do some delving into our unconscious mind. Think of an iceberg. You can see the conscious mind as the tip of the iceberg—one tenth of the whole. The other nine-tenths represent the unconscious mind and it is here that we find negative traits and issues that we have disowned, denied and generally not accepted as part of our make-up.

In an effort to effect change, you need to raise the iceberg out of the water a little. In other words, you need to become consciously aware of things you have problems with. Then it is possible to choose how to behave because you are in control of yourself, rather than being controlled by your unconscious mind. Once you have noticed and accepted important issues, you have started the process of individual change.

GETTING STARTED

Taking into account these aspects of change—of change being scary, and of needing to become more aware of yourself—do you feel ready to begin the process of changing yourself?

Change is a process that requires an investment of effort and energy. You need to be able to give it the attention it requires and you should set some time aside for this. For example, it takes about a month of focusing on a new behaviour until it becomes more of a habitual behaviour. So, if you are practising a new behaviour every day, then you need to allow a month of conscious thinking about it.

There is no time like the present to start the change process.

USING THIS BOOK TO START YOUR CHANGE PROCESS

Take a moment now to think about how you might change and keep it in mind as you continue your journey through this book. Do you think that you will be willing to begin the process of changing then? It will help the whole process if you manage to carry out the suggested exercises, either by yourself or with a friend.

The processes of change that you use depend on the kind of problem and the approaches that work best for you. This book details some techniques for change that can be done alone. However, if you find that a technique doesn't work after you have tried it on a number of occasions, then perhaps it is better to have some help. We cannot always deal with our problems alone. It can be helpful, therefore, to seek help from an appropriate professional.

As you read through the chapters you might well start to discover things in yourself that you would like to change. Chapter 7 shows you how to set goals in order to start to this process. You will probably find it most useful to finish the book and then work out what goals you want to set for a better future.

SUMMARY

- Deciding to change is a big decision.
- It is about taking charge of yourself and your life.
- It can be scary to think about change, but the process does not change who you are deep down. You will still be you.
- Change happens by taking different, small steps in the present.
- The mind is a powerful tool to effect change.
- There is no time like the present to start the process.
- Change takes effort, energy and time.
- We can only change ourselves, not others.

CHAPTER 2
TAKING RESPONSIBILITY

One of the most important steps in getting ready to change is to take responsibility for yourself. As adults, we are expected to be responsible for ourselves—for our behaviour, thoughts and emotions in both our personal and working lives. But being responsible to the extent that we can acknowledge our problems and our role in shaping our lives is not always straightforward. This chapter discusses issues of taking responsibility and describes how to do it.

BLAMING OTHERS VERSUS TAKING RESPONSIBILITY

Taking responsibility can present a number of challenges to us as individuals. It can seem easier, and even logical, to blame other people and things when we find ourselves in a problematic situation.

Some people may blame their parents or their partner. Others may see an event, or drugs, as the cause of their problems. This is the victim stance. It says, "Look. Poor me. I couldn't help it." The victim stance avoids addressing our own part in the situation. For instance, we may allow others to make decisions for us, respond violently to painful situations, or run away from difficulties rather than face them. Until we realise and accept that we have a role in our life circumstances, we cannot work out what we can do to improve them. We need to understand ourselves as having the capacity to act and make choices before we can choose to do things differently.

There are of course some circumstances, especially when a crime has been committed, when the victim is right to blame the perpetrator. This is a different issue from taking responsibility for yourself in everyday life situations.

THE POWER OF CHOICE

It is a very powerful moment when people realise that it is possible to make choices about how they live their lives, and that it is possible to choose alternate ways of thinking and acting.

This can happen when we take responsibility for at least a part (if not all) of our circumstances. Remember, however, that taking responsibility is a process of small steps—you don't have to take responsibility for everything all at once. It is also important to take responsibility only for decisions that you are in charge of.

It can be difficult to reach the position of taking responsibility. For some people, it may just seem easier to stay the same. Change involves work and it can seem rather scary to take charge of yourself and deal with the consequences of making new choices. For instance, if you decide to take a different path to the people you currently see as your friends, you may not be able to continue the friendship in the same way. However, you can choose to accept the consequences of your new choices.

NOT BLAMING THE PAST

There is no point in blaming yourself for what happened in the past while you were growing up. At the time, you probably made some decisions that seemed okay, given your age and the situation you were in, but that you now regret. While those ways of behaving or thinking may not seem appropriate in hindsight, you now have the opportunity to decide what is right for you as an adult and a responsible person.

Nor is there any point in blaming your parents, your friends, or your teachers, for their influence in the past. When you were young, you had little choice about this. But now that you are an adult, can think more independently, and have become more self-reliant, you have the opportunity to do things differently.

It can be helpful to understand that while things may not have been good in the past, people generally do the best with what they have. Blaming yourself for past actions is not going to change the past, but you can change how you feel and think about it. You may find that as you start accepting the past and working towards change, you have some difficult emotions to deal with (see chapter 8).

KNOWLEDGE VERSUS ACTION

There is a difference between knowing in your head what you should do, and actually doing it. It's the putting into practice stage that we can have a problem with.

Sometimes this problem may be caused by conflicts between values or beliefs (see chapters 4 and 5). For instance, if you have a belief that you are not very good at doing something, then you are less likely to try it. Or it could be a matter of old patterns of behaving taking control of you, almost daring you to do things differently. All the old reasons and excuses can suck you in again.

It will take courage and work to put new learned behaviours into action when old behaviours are so much more comfortable and familiar. You will need to constantly push against what was learned so well in the past and is now virtually automatic behaviour.

TAKING OWNERSHIP OF A PROBLEM

Perhaps other people have been encouraging you to change your behaviour but you don't see the need. It is a fact that we can fool ourselves 100% of the time, but it is impossible to fool others that much or for that long. You need to be able to accept that there is a problem somewhere and that it is within your control.

Some people will find it easier to acknowledge the ownership of a problem than others. Again, it is about taking responsibility. Until you can say, "That is my problem," then how can you fix it?

If you accept responsibility for your part in your life, and can see yourself as the agent of change, then you are ready to start to make changes. If you stop blaming others for your predicaments, then you can get on with the process of changing what happens by putting your goals for change into action.

SUMMARY

- While you are blaming others, you see yourself as a victim and are unable to take charge of your life.

- You need to take responsibility for yourself and your part in your life experience.

- When you choose to accept responsibility, then you are able to start the process of change.

- Some people have a problem with putting what they know into practice. It does not happen without a lot of conscious choice and effort.

- We can't change the past, but we can change our perceptions of past events and experiences.

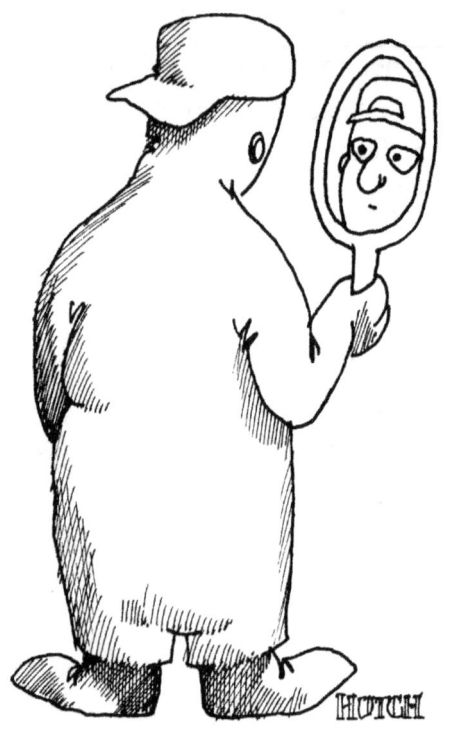

SELF-MONITORING

CHAPTER 3
OBSERVING YOURSELF

Observing how you act and interact helps you to identify what you need to change. It also helps you to monitor the changes that you are putting into practice. You may already be aware of yourself in this way, or you may need to train yourself to become more aware of your thoughts, emotions and reactions. This chapter describes what observing yourself involves and shows how you can use what you learn from this to make changes.

GETTING INTO THE OBSERVER ROLE

The first step is to be aware. In order to become a good observer of yourself, it is important to take a further step backwards. That is, **to be aware of being aware**. What is happening in this state of mind is just observing. Not judging. Observing who says what, what happens then, and what happens next. Your focus is just the sequence of events.

Whether in a situation by yourself or with others, what you observe of yourself is your verbal and behavioural responses, including thoughts and feelings. What you are able to observe of other people is their verbal and visual responses. Psychologists call this self-monitoring.

MONITORING YOURSELF IN VARIOUS SITUATIONS

Self-monitoring helps you become aware of how you behave in different situations. For instance, if you have problems generally with people in authority, then whenever you come into contact with those people you need to go into observation mode. Observe how you communicate with them—look at how you act and respond, and their reactions and responses to you. What is it that happens?

What you learn from this observation can help you to identify what you want to change. For example, you may wish you had more time for yourself. However, you may find through monitoring situations with your friends and family that you always say "Yes" when they ask you to do something for them or take part in activities with them, even when you don't have time or don't want to. The first step in this instance is to say "No" more often. You can then monitor what happens when you say "No."

One of my clients was in a situation like this and her experience shows how monitoring can also help you put changes into practice. On one occasion she was invited to go to a function by a friend. She felt tired and thought it would be boring. Her first thought was to go, but she managed to pull herself up and say no, that she wasn't able to attend that night. Her friend, she said later, seemed a bit surprised but accepted the situation and my client was very pleased with the outcome. She gave herself a big pat on the back for being able to say no and it gave her confidence to continue.

USING SELF-TALK

Self-monitoring is supported by what is sometimes called self-talk. For example, when you draw a square, you have in your head the rules of how to draw a square, and as you are in the process of drawing the square you tell yourself how to do it, or what to watch for.

This is self-talk. And self-talk can be negative, positive or neutral. Drawing the square as described above is an example of neutral self-talk. It does not involve judging anything. However, if you said to yourself after you had tried to draw a square, "That's not a square, stupid!" then that is negative self-talk. On the other hand, if you said to yourself, "That is a good square," then that is positive self-talk.

Self-talk is something we do all the time. Negative self-talk puts you down and works against your capacity to change, so try to reduce it. On the other hand, you can harness positive and neutral self-talk to help the change process. Neutral self-talk is your observations as you monitor yourself, and positive self-talk works as self-encouragement. My client used positive self-talk to encourage herself to say, "No" to her friend who wanted her to go out.

OBSERVING EMOTIONS

Another useful thing is to observe feelings and to describe the exact emotion you are feeling when you are self-monitoring, and indeed at other times. Also, see if you can identify correctly the emotions that others are experiencing. There is a list of emotions in the following table. Selective use of these words will help you to convey more accurately how you are feeling.

Emotions

Abandoned	Cruel	Frantic
Adequate	Crushed	Frustrated
Adamant	Culpable	Frightened
Affectionate	Deceitful	Free
Agony	Defeated	Full
Almighty	Delighted	Fury
Ambivalent	Depressed	Gay
Angry	Desirous	Glad
Annoyed	Despair	Good
Anxious	Destructive	Gratified
Apathetic	Determined	Gratitude
Astounded	Different	Greedy
Awed	Diffident	Grief
Bad	Diminished	Groovy
Beautiful	Disappointed	Guilty
Betrayed	Discontented	Gullible
Bitter	Distracted	Happy
Blissful	Divided	Hate
Bold	Dominated	Heavenly
Bored	Dubious	Helpful
Brave	Eager	Helpless
Burdened	Ecstatic	High
Calm	Electrified	Homesick
Capable	Embarrassed	Honoured
Captivated	Empty	Hopeful
Challenged	Enchanted	Horrible
Charmed	Energetic	Hurt
Cheated	Enervated	Hysterical
Cheerful	Enjoy	Ignored
Childish	Envious	Immortal
Clever	Excited	Imposed upon
Combative	Evil	Impressed
Competitive	Exasperated	Infatuated
Condemned	Exhausted	Infuriated
Confused	Fascinated	Inspired
Conspicuous	Fawning	Intimidated
Contented	Flustered	Isolated
Contrite	Foolish	Jealous

Emotions

Joyous
Jumpy
Kicky
Kind
Keen
Laconic
Lazy
Lecherous
Licentious
Lonely
Longing
Loving
Low
Lustful
Mad
Maudlin
Mean
Melancholy
Miserable
Mystical
Naughty
Nervous
Nice
Nutty
Obnoxious
Obsessed
Odd
Opposed
Outraged
Overwhelmed
Pain
Panicky
Parsimonious
Peaceful
Persecuted
Petrified
Pity
Pleasant

Pleased
Precarious
Pressured
Pretty
Prim
Prissy
Proud
Quarrelsome
Queer
Rage
Rapture
Refreshed
Rejected
Relaxed
Relieved
Remorse
Restless
Reverent
Rewarded
Righteous
Sad
Sated
Satisfied
Scared
Screwed up
Servile
Settled
Sexy
Shame
Shocked
Silly
Sceptical
Sneaky
Solemn
Sorrowful
Spiteful
Startled
Stingy

Strange
Snuffed
Stupid
Stunned
Stupefied
Sure
Sympathetic
Talkative
Tempted
Tenacious
Tenuous
Tense
Tentative
Terrible
Terrified
Threatened
Tired
Thwarted
Trapped
Troubled
Trusting
Ugly
Understanding
Uneasy
Unsettled
Upset
Violent
Vehement
Vital/Vitality
Vulnerable
Vivacious
Wicked
Wonderful
Weepy
Worried
Zany

OBSERVING YOUR INTERACTIONS WITH OTHERS

Many problems arise through misinterpretation, but in fact these are just mistakes in sending and receiving messages and it is possible to reduce them.

A number of factors may influence the outcome of a conversation between two people. Being aware of these can help you to observe and manage your interactions for better outcomes.

One factor is the extent to which you and the person you are talking with have a shared understanding of the meaning of words. It can be surprising how many shades of meaning there are. If the other person has misinterpreted your meaning, it is possible that the words you used meant something different to them.

Another factor, and a particularly important one, is that each of you comes to the conversation with your own personal history, attitudes, beliefs, and values. These act as a partial filter to how you understand each other and you can find that the person you are talking to has not interpreted what you have said in the way you intended. For instance, the person you are talking with may have a negative frame of mind. This might mean that what you say is misinterpreted to be negative, when in fact you did not mean it that way.

Other factors that contribute to how a person picks up what you are saying include how you speak, your tone of voice, and the gestures you use. All of these are in your control and you can adjust them to fit the situation, just as you can try to be as clear as possible in your choice of words and so choose words that you know the other person will understand.

By watching someone's responses to what you are saying, you can get some idea about whether you are getting your message across. This includes watching their emotional response to what you say, as well as listening to their verbal response. Are their emotions obvious or not obvious? What particular emotion do you think they might be feeling from their verbal response to you?

WORKING ON GETTING THE MESSAGE ACROSS

If the other person's response indicates that they did not get the message, then you need to explain further what you mean, or to qualify what you are saying. You can also try using different words to describe what you mean or explain what you mean in a different way. And don't be afraid to check if the other person has understood what you are trying to say. It is also good to confirm that you are interpreting what others are saying correctly. People will respect your concern for wanting to get things right.

Perhaps one of the most important things in getting your message across is to avoid using words that inflame or upset the other person. There are a number of good texts around that explain how to go about this.

IDEAS FOR RESPONDING TO UPSETTING COMMUNICATION SITUATIONS

Let's suppose that you are working on a goal of not allowing minor things to upset you, even though in the past you haven't really seen them as minor. If someone says to you something like, "Not today," and you would rather have an answer right now, then maybe you can create a sentence you can say to yourself to help you from getting upset (or becoming less upset as before).

- What about telling yourself that you need to remind the person first thing in the morning so that there is all day for them to find out the answer?

- What about saying to yourself that this person is having a bad day today and hopefully tomorrow will be better?

- What about saying to yourself that if you keep on asking and are persistent then eventually you may get an answer? It might just depend on the person you are asking and how much information is available at the time.

You can say all these things to yourself to help you to reduce how upset you might be feeling.

UNDERSTANDING THE DIFFERENCE BETWEEN PASSIVE, AGGRESSIVE AND ASSERTIVE

It is important to be able to label communications more or less correctly in terms of whether you or others are acting in a passive, assertive or aggressive manner.

Being passive involves complying and agreeing to someone else's assessment or statement in a situation, sometimes out of fear. It's allowing others to have power over you.

Aggression involves using a tone of voice or physical manner that is threatening to others. The aggressor has the power over the person being threatened.

Being assertive is behaving in a way that is accepting of both yourself and others, and where there is collaborative power.

ORIENTING TO THE PRESENT MOMENT

If you have been observing how you operate in terms of the past, present and future (as discussed in chapter 1) and have discovered that you are not very often in the present, then you can do the following exercise.

Examine what you are doing at a particular moment. "I am sitting in this chair and I am thinking x, and seeing y, and I am feeling confused/angry/sad," or whatever emotion you are feeling. Be aware of your senses, including checking whether your muscles are tight, tense or relaxed. If you do this exercise a few times a day, you become a little more tuned in to how you and your body are feeling in the present moment. Some people go through life without really being aware of their body, except when it comes to feeling the good stuff. You should at least be able to feel your heartbeat. That is a reasonable sign. If you are not aware of your heart pumping your blood around your body, then get in touch immediately! It might be a sign that you are not in touch with your emotions at all. At the same time, you should know or have some idea about which emotions you are most in touch with.

KEEPING A JOURNAL

It is a good idea to keep a daily record of how you are dealing with the variety of situations you are monitoring. It is better to write things down as you go through the day, but this is not always possible. Write down the same evening, in a special exercise book or a small notebook or diary, what happened during the day, what you noticed about the situations, your responses to others and their responses to you.

What were your thoughts, and feelings, and actions, and the sequence of these? What was the result? Do you think that the other people would have felt okay about what happened? Would you have preferred to have acted differently? Writing all these answers down will be helpful.

Keep observing for a time and note down the areas that you seem to have most difficulty with in your targeted interactions. Identify a range of approaches to the problem area. Work out what your preferred result would be in relation to your intention for this interaction. What might work better next time? Sometimes it might just be a matter of not reacting immediately, but taking time to think. Creating or finding a new perspective may occur when there is space or some distance from being in the experience versus seeing the interaction from a different angle.

SUMMARY

- In order to find out what you want to change and how to do so, you need to explore your current situation. This is where you are right now.

- Self-monitoring involves taking a step backwards and observing, but not judging, the sequence of events within a situation over an interaction. Observe the thoughts, feelings and behaviours that you have. Look at the responses of others to what you do and say.

- It is important to make your message clear. You can always check with others to make sure that they understood what you were trying to tell them.

- The way to get your message across is to not blame the other person for any problem. Attack the problem, not the person.

- Self-monitoring is an ongoing process throughout the day.

- Think about whether the emotional words that you use are actually what you feel. Expand your vocabulary in this area.

- Express the emotion, even if this only involves saying it to yourself. This labels it and allows it to go.

- Keeping a journal or diary in relation to what you are monitoring is helpful for later reference and for sorting out and getting clear about what occurs when you encounter problem situations.

CHAPTER 4
SORTING OUT VALUES

You probably picked up this book because you have said to yourself, on at least one level, that you are interested in changing something in your life. You may be dissatisfied with the way things are going at present. You may want to achieve something that you have not yet managed to do. Sorting out what is important to you—your values—is an essential part of making changes.

This chapter includes background information about personal values and practical ideas for working out which values are most important to you.

WHAT IS A VALUE?

When we say we value something, we are describing its importance and meaning to us. When psychologists talk about personal values, they are referring to the guiding principles of our lives.

We learn values through our families, education, society and our life experiences. Values are not in themselves right or wrong—they are what we see as important. When it comes to a time of making changes in our life directions, it makes sense to take stock of the values we have picked up along the way.

WHAT ARE YOUR VALUES?

Values can be abstract concepts until we start to think about our own personal values and the application of them in our lives. The following table provides a list of values with a description of what it means in practice, and a column for you to rate how important that value is to you. You can download extra copies from my website.

This list is by no means complete—you might like to add to it. These were suggested by Rokeach (1968).

Value	Description	Your rating (1-10)
Achievement	Sense of accomplishment	
Aesthetics	Enjoying and contributing to beautiful things, nature, the arts	
Challenge	Trying something new or demanding	
Companionship	Caring, close and intimate relationships, family/friends	
Community	Having neighbours, active in local affairs	
Competitiveness	Winning, taking risks, pitting self against others	
Contentment	Inner harmony, having peace of mind, emotional health	
Cooperation	Working with others, teamwork	
Creativity	Being imaginative, innovative in any field	
Excitement	Stimulation, fast pace, novelty	
Financial Security	Steady, adequate income	
Forgiving	Willing to forgive others	
Freedom	Independence, free choice	
Helpfulness	Assisting others, improving society, being needed	
Integrity	Honesty, sincerity, standing up for your beliefs and principles	
Involvement	Participating with others, belonging, joining in activities with others	
Intellectual Stimulation	Learning, discussing, seeking truth, information and understanding	
Leadership	Having authority, influence over others	
Loyalty	Being faithful to certain people or causes	

Value	Description	Your rating (1-10)
Morality	Living according to your moral/ethical beliefs	
Order	Routine, stability, conformity	
Personal Growth	Using all of your potential	
Pleasure	Fun, laughter, leisurely lifestyle, enjoyment, joy	
Physical Health	Freedom from pain, disease, disability	
Physical Challenge	Strength, speed, endurance, agility	
Recognition	Status, respect from others	
Responsibility	Dependable, reliable	
Self-control	Restrained, self-disciplined	
Self-reliance	Self-sufficient	
Self-respect	Self-esteem	
Solitude	Quiet, space, being alone, doing things alone	
Time Freedom	Not having a strict schedule or timetable	
Tranquillity	Avoiding pressures	
Spirituality	Strong religious beliefs, connectedness to the spiritual	
Prosperity	Making money, being rich	
Wisdom	Understanding life, discovering knowledge and meaning	
Variety	New, different and changing activities and places	

As a way of starting to think about your values, go down the list and rate each of them between 1 and 10, where 1 is not important at all, and 10 is extremely important. Think about them in relation to your life. How important is each? After you have gone through and rated each value, work out your top 5. Sometimes it will be very difficult to get it down to 5, but try just the same. You might get it down to the top 6. The more you can narrow it down, the better.

When you have done this, go through the list again and see if there are any values there that you would like to make more important in your life.

THE VALUE OF VALUES

Values help to define how you live your life. They simplify the decision-making process when you are faced with many choices because they enable you to ask the question, "Which of these choices or paths would help me to uphold those values I believe are important?" Choices are easier when you see a path in which your values will be fulfilled.

You can make both major and minor decisions on the basis of your values. The greater awareness you have of yourself and how you want to live your life, the easier it will be to make day-to-day decisions, whether important or not. The ideal state to get to is to know that you can live with the consequences of every decision that you make.

LIVING YOUR VALUES

There are many different ways of living by the values that are important to you. For example, if respect is one of your values you can show respect to others by allowing them to speak without interrupting, and by being polite, both of which are then also likely to generate respect in return. On the other hand, if you were a member of a gang there might be very specific ways of showing respect to other members.

Another example is when two people have achievement as a high rating value; one may see it as being able to achieve high marks while doing a degree, while the other may see it as being able to achieve a lot in a day.

When you identify the values that are important to you, you then have the opportunity to choose the way you would like to live them. For instance, if spirituality is high on your list, one way of fulfilling it could be by going to church. Another could be by going for country walks or watching nature programs on television.

The way you live your values is an expression of your individuality. It might be of interest to find out what others see as their top 5 values. Compare their values with what you know about the person; there is usually some sort of match.

Like everything, the values you live by may change as you go through life. Some values become more important and the order in which you rank them may change. It is a good idea to reflect on your values every now and then as a way of keeping in touch with changes in your life and yourself.

WORKING ON YOUR VALUES

Once you've identified values that are important to you, it's time to start working on them. This is really quite simple.

For instance, because we are social beings many people may have love and companionship high on their list. If you do, then you should start working on your close relationships on a daily basis.

Think of integrity as another example. If this is high on your list, then it means that you want to be honest and work within your personal boundaries and ethics. To actually fulfil this value, you need to maintain that honesty in everyday life by, for instance, carrying out what you say you will do.

RULES ASSOCIATED WITH VALUES

During your life so far, you may have come across rules or statements that you still live by. An example might be to respect your elders. Such statements are generally related to values and you may find that the ones you grew up with are associated with the values that are important to you now. On the other hand, you may find that they are not positive or helpful ways of living.

Think about whether you use any rules like this. Things that your parents used to say, perhaps. What are they? Are they at all helpful for you or for others?

You may and can choose your own values and rules to live by. However, it is important to accept some values that exist within your local society so that you do not come into conflict with it. Laws are based on values. Generally, if your values include relating well with people, then the consequences should be positive.

POSITIVE RULES ABOUT INTERACTION WITH PEOPLE

In thinking about positive and beneficial rules to live by, if you were to have only one rule in your life, then it might be something like, "Treat others as you would like to be treated." This sets the ground for treating others with respect, compassion and empathy.

I have come across a number of people who seem to work on a rule that says, "I treat others as they treat me." This is all very well, but certainly does not take into account the fact that it is possible to misinterpret others' behaviour. If you think you are being treated with disrespect and you behave in the same manner back to that person and to others, then the consequence of this behaviour would be that you would be treated disrespectfully. So, people who use this rule end up in a negative spiral that continues downwards. To start a more positive spiral, treat others in the way you would like to be treated in every respect, and others will treat you a lot better. You will also find that your attitude becomes more positive and that you end up believing more positive things about people due to your experience.

Again, the idea is to take responsibility for yourself and your behaviour so others can too. You can start the process.

Another positive rule that you could adopt is one that the Dalai Lama suggests: "To not intentionally harm another." It is up to you as to how you define another, whether as human or human/animal/being. By not intentionally harming another, then you will be acting within societal laws as well as ethical and moral laws.

MYTHICAL RULES

In talking about rules, it is also important to talk about the rules that people often think are in existence, but do not exist. There are two of these to be aware of.

Good things happen to good people and thus bad things happen to bad people. There is no evidence that shows this occurs and no rule in relation to this. Both good and bad things happen to people whoever they are. Events may happen, but the judgement about whether it is good or bad is made by people. A negative event in no way means that the person deserved it. That is a judgement.

The world is a just or fair place. There is no rule written that states everything has to be fair—it would be nice if everyone were treated fairly but it doesn't always happen. There is also no rule saying that justice has to prevail. We might like it to, but that is all.

There is no rule that says the world should be a certain way. When you catch yourself thinking along the lines of these above myths, then you can remind yourself that they are just myths. And then move on.

SUMMARY

- Values are the guiding principles of our lives.

- It is helpful to know which things you value or feel are important to you. There are no right or wrong values.

- Values change over your life and it is good to review them regularly.

- Values are gained through society, childhood, family, and experiences.

- It is important to have values and to live by rules that include them.

- Two good rules are to treat others as you would like to be treated, and to not intentionally harm another.

- However, there are no rules that say how the world should be: it is a myth that the world is a just or fair place, and that good things happen to good people.

CHAPTER 5
SORTING OUT CORE BELIEFS

We often associate beliefs with belief in a god, or with something like a conviction that the sun will rise tomorrow. The beliefs that are relevant to self-change are personal beliefs about how we see ourselves, others and the world around us. These are often called core beliefs. As with personal values, these beliefs are the basis for many of our decisions and actions, as well as the way we relate to others. Sorting out what you believe about yourself and considering how this affects your life is an important step in the process of change.

This chapter shows how you can identify and develop positive ways of seeing yourself and managing your life. It provides an overview and examples of core beliefs, and highlights the problem of negative beliefs. It also discusses two important ways of thinking about yourself and others that you may need to work on to achieve the changes you want to make.

OVERVIEW OF THE CORE BELIEFS

A core belief is what you see as true or real. However, when you think about it, it may only be true for you, not for other people. We all have a set of beliefs that act as a filter through which we see the world and understand reality. We develop these beliefs from our own experience and through what we have been told.

Individuals often have different beliefs about the meaning of a situation. For instance, some people see having to speak in public as a scary thing to do because they believe they are not competent or worthy. Someone who believes in their own self-worth and competence will probably regard it more as a challenge. However, it could be that we have this belief because we do not have the practice and skill right now, which we could improve on. These different beliefs result in different consequences; the person who sees themselves as incompetent will probably avoid speaking and thus lose out on any benefits they may be gained, while the one who regards it as a challenge will take it up and have the opportunity to gain further self-confidence and knowledge.

This example shows how your core beliefs impact on your life for better or worse, so getting to know your beliefs and how they work in your life is a major step in working towards change.

The following list of ten core beliefs, based on McKay and Fanning (1991), is a good place to start the process of sorting out your beliefs.

1. that you are at least as worthy as other people—**self-esteem**

2. that you are generally safe as you go about your daily life—**safety**

3. that you are competent—**competency**

4. that you are in control—**control**

5. that you are lovable—**lovability**

6. that you have personal freedom to make choices—**autonomy**

7. that you are treated fairly—**justice**

8. that you belong—**belonging**

9. that people are trustworthy and generally good—**trust**

10. that you can expect the same of others as of yourself—**standards**

SORTING OUT HOW THE CORE BELIEFS WORK IN YOUR LIFE.

You will probably see straight away that it is far better to be on the positive side of these beliefs than to be on the negative. For instance, if you believe that you are unsafe, you are going to be fearful wherever you are and wherever you go. It is not a good space to be in and can restrict your life considerably.

You will also see that there is often a connection between different beliefs. If you veer towards the negative on one, then you may also be on the negative side in one or more of the others. For instance, if you do not believe that you are worthwhile, what do you believe about being loved, or belonging, or being free to make your own choices in life? If you believe that you are not safe, then you are not likely to trust others very much, or to believe that you are justly treated.

This section discusses each of the core beliefs as a guide to understanding how they may be working in your life. For each core belief there are also some questions that will help you to identify where you might be on the scale between positive and negative in relation to particular beliefs. Once you have identified where you stand on the core beliefs, you will be able to see where you could work on achieving a more positive outlook. What this means is that you will value yourself more.

Self-esteem

Questions to ask yourself:

- Do you feel that you deserve to have good things happen to you?

- Would you expect the good things to continue over time?

- Would you accept the good things as being for ever, or have you found yourself in the past messing up the good things because you knew they could never last?

- Do nice events have a use-by date?

If you have high self-esteem and believe that you are worthy, you are more likely to operate in your world in a confident manner and achieve a lot. You will also feel that you deserve good things to happen to you and that they will probably last.

If you have low self-esteem, then you are going to interpret the things that you see, hear and feel from the view that you are essentially no good. You will not hear compliments when they are meant as such. You will not see people looking at you admiringly, and will interpret their looks as negative rather than positive. And you will believe that the situations you come across are against you rather than for you. You might also think that you have to strive much harder than others to get people to like you. People with low self-esteem often believe that they are not worthy of good things and that anything good that happens probably will not last.

Do you think it would be helpful to improve your self-esteem?

Safety

Questions to ask yourself:

- How safe do you generally feel going about your daily life?

- Do you feel that the world is a dangerous place in general or specifically?

- What does it mean if it is dangerous? And how dangerous is this?

- Is it just dangerous over there (wherever there is)?

The important thing is that you are able to go about your daily life in a relatively relaxed way rather than feeling unsafe from moment to moment.

People may lose their belief of being safe after a traumatic event. If you identify safety as an issue for you, it is likely that you will be able to work through the experience that has caused your fear and come to believe that you are safe. You may need some skilled support to help you in this process.

Competency

Questions to ask yourself:

- Do you feel that you are at least as competent as other people are?

- Do you feel competent in at least one or two areas?

If you feel that you are competent, then you should feel self-confident enough to be willing to try new things. If you are skilled in one or more areas, then it is likely that you feel competent in those areas too. There is an important overlap between believing that you are competent and self-esteem. The more areas you feel competent in, the higher your self-esteem will probably be.

When you don't feel competent in certain spheres of activity, you probably avoid participating in them. A good starting point for developing confidence in new areas is believing that you are competent in daily living—for example in the work that you do, or in relating to people.

Control

Questions to ask yourself:

- Do you feel that you are the one who is helping your life along?

- Can you make decisions that affect your life and put them into action?

- Do you accept the consequences of these decisions?

- Do you feel that you are controlling other people?

- Do you feel out of control in your behaviour?

If you believe that you are in control, then you feel that you can instigate changes that you want in your life. You are in charge of you and your life.

If you feel you are controlling other adults, then you may like to investigate your motives for doing this. In controlling others, you are forcing them to behave in ways that you want them to, and this takes away autonomy and choice for those people. This situation means that they are likely to resent you or have other negative feelings towards you. Is this what you want?

Are there aspects of your life that seem to be taking you over? If you feel out of control or not in control, then you might feel helpless and at the mercy of others. Making the positive choice to work towards greater control is an important first step in taking charge of your situation.

Lovability

Questions to ask yourself:

- Do you feel that you are lovable?

- What qualities do you have that enable you to accept this?

- If you feel that you are unlovable, then what qualities do you have that mean you don't deserve to be loved?

If you reject being lovable, you might be disregarding important aspects and qualities that you have that do actually make you lovable. If you feel that you are lovable, then you are likely to have positive relationships with people, including sexual relationships.

If you feel that you are unlovable, then you may avoid seeking a partner and also avoid social interaction. Additionally, you are likely to interpret what others may say to you in a negative way. For instance, if someone invites you to go out, you may think they are doing this so they can make fun of you. If you don't rate your lovability very highly, you may also have low self-esteem.

If you reject being lovable, you might be disregarding the very qualities that do make you lovable. Therefore, acknowledging these qualities could be a good way to start believing that you are lovable.

Autonomy

Questions to ask yourself:

- Do you feel that you have the freedom to make choices?

- Do you feel that you are able to make up your own mind?

- Do you feel that your choices are controlled by another person?

If you believe that you have autonomy, then you feel you are free to make your own choices, make up your own mind, and not be controlled by other people.

If you don't feel that you have autonomy, then you may feel controlled by others. If you are low on autonomy, then you are also likely to be low on control.

Justice

Questions to ask yourself:

- Do you feel that you are treated fairly?

- Do you feel that other people get more in life than you do?

- Do you accept it when you don't get what you want?

- Do you feel that everything works out all right in the end?

If you feel that you are treated fairly in general, and that you have enough in life, then you are on the positive side of this belief. What you get in life you see as reasonable.

If you feel that you are not treated fairly, then it is likely that you see circumstances, or other people, working against you.

Belonging

Questions to ask yourself:

- Do you feel that you belong to your family?

- Do you feel that you belong to your social group?

- Do you feel that you belong to your community?

- Do you feel that you belong to your country?

- Do you feel that you belong to the human race?

If you feel that you belong to your family, social group, community, country and the human race, then you are likely to feel secure and connected. Belonging is a sense of being comfortable, fitting in, and relating with others.

If you feel that you don't belong to one or more of these groups, then you are likely to feel different in some way. Maybe you feel on some level that you don't fit in. If you want to work on making stronger connections with people, a good starting point is to find a group that you can join where you learn something, or to engage in a hobby activity.

If you want to feel more connected to your family, you could investigate your descendants and work out your family history. Finding members of your birth family may be of value if you are adopted. It is best to consult relevant support organisations before embarking on this journey.

It is a fact that, no matter what, you belong to the human race.

Trust

Questions to ask yourself:

- Do you feel that people in general are okay and try to do the right thing?

- Do you feel that other people are generally out to get you?

- Do you feel that other people generally don't care about others?

- Do you feel that you are able to trust others in a general sense?

- Are you able to trust others with anything?

- Can you trust others to at least act in a reasonably human fashion?

- Do you feel you can trust yourself to act upon what you want or decide?

If you are able to trust yourself and others in a general sense, then it is easier to live your life in a relaxed way. If you think that people usually do the right thing, that no-one is out to get you, and that you can broadly trust others, then this is positive. Some people might trust others too much and get into problems because of this. For instance, in a high-tech world we need to be careful of internet scams and the like.

If you aren't able to trust others even in a general sense, and if you think others are out to get you, then this is not a good place to be. You are likely to avoid interacting with others and you are also likely to believe that you are not treated fairly. Working on trust will probably also involve working on your beliefs in justice and your own competency.

Standards

Questions to ask yourself:

- Do you expect more of yourself than you do of others?

- Or do you expect more of others than you do of yourself?

- Are you able to be compassionate towards yourself and others?

- Do you feel that you are able to make mistakes and learn from them?

- Do you feel that others can learn from mistakes too?

If you have the same expectations of others as of yourself and are able to be compassionate towards yourself and others, then you are likely to judge your actions and those of others in a compassionate manner.

If you have high expectations of others and fairly rigid standards of behaviour for yourself and others, then it is likely that you judge both yourself and others harshly.

For instance, if you have high expectations of others, you may find they often don't meet your expectations and you criticise them. This may strain your relationships.

WORKING ON CORE BELIEFS

Once you have worked out which core beliefs you would like to improve, you can select ways of working on them from the following techniques. It is best to work on one belief at a time, and just use one technique at a time.

Use of affirmations

An affirmation is a short statement that is expressed only in positive words. This means there are no "Nots", or negations of a state or word. For instance, if you say to yourself, "Do not think of a pink elephant," you have to think of a pink elephant before you can cross it out. It is better to say, "Think of a grey elephant," if this is what you were after in the first place.

Repeating affirmations is helpful in developing more positive beliefs. You can repeat them over 20 times a day. Saying them in front of a mirror can increase the effectiveness of self-worth affirmations. A good self-worth affirmation to start with is, "I accept myself as I am." Another is, "I approve of myself."

Start with an affirmation that you can almost believe at first, then once you feel you do believe it, work your way up to one that is harder to believe in. The idea is to reprogram your brain. As well as lots of repetition, more positive experiences will help achieve this. For instance, if you work on the belief of competence by repeating the affirmation, "I am as competent as other people," and then manage to try something new, practice it and become better at it, your rating of this belief will improve. So, begin with one small step forward at a time. Look at the chapter on goal setting (chapter 7) and develop a progressive list of affirmations to work through that is just for you. Then work through them slowly. Louise Hay (1984) provides a list of affirmations that you might like to use.

Counteractive statements

Whenever you think a negative thought, as in negative self-talk (see chapter 3), then you could think up a positive statement that will be powerful enough to cancel the negative self-talk. This is another way of deprogramming yourself and your beliefs. Again, it is important to be persistent. Don't give up if it doesn't work immediately. Your beliefs have been around for some time so they might well take a lot of time and effort to shift. Think up your very own statements and repeat them often to yourself whenever negative self-talk comes into play.

For example, if you are low on the core belief of competence, you may not like doing things you haven't done before. Your negative self-talk might be, "I won't be able to set up this Ikea pack. I'll mess it up and then I'll look foolish." Therefore, you could try a sentence like, "If I follow the instructions, I should be able to do it. It's all a matter of fitting bits in. I can take my time." Remember that the counteractive statement should be strong enough to overcome the negative self-talk.

Investigating the past

The basis for many of our beliefs is in past experiences. For each core belief you are low on, McKay and Fanning (1991) suggest the following exercise: write down the age you were, the event, and whether it has resulted in a positive or negative outcome in relation to the core belief. Doing this exercise for as many events as you can recall may help you come up with a new way of thinking about your beliefs. For instance, you may find that there is no basis in the reality of your past experiences to lead you to have a negative belief about yourself. Perhaps you can remember at age 4 being told that you did a good painting. This would be positive for self-esteem. Again, at age 8 maybe you can remember being teased. This could be negative for your self-esteem. So, keep on collecting experiences until you have a number of them. If you have more positive experiences than negative, you could improve your self-esteem rating and the way you think about yourself.

If you have experienced past traumatic events, then it would be best if you do not do this exercise and seek expert help in processing these events.

Refer to McKay and Fanning (1991) for more ways to investigate your beliefs.

WAYS OF THINKING AND 'BEING IN THE WORLD'

As well as core beliefs, other ways of thinking about yourself and the world can have an important effect on the way you live your life. Two very influential ways of thinking are discussed below. If you can work out where you stand on these you may find positive things that you can do about them.

I'M OKAY, YOU'RE OKAY

If you believe that others are basically good, but you are essentially not good, then you get the position of, "You're okay, I'm not okay," that Eric Berne (1964) talks about, and is highlighted in his theory of Transactional Analysis. Of course, the best position is, "I'm okay and you're okay."

If others are not seen as okay, then the position is, "I'm okay, you're not okay." Neither of these unequal stances, nor the position, "I'm not okay and you're not okay," are healthy for functioning in a logical, reasonable adult fashion.

Transactional Analysis also points out the victim/persecutor/rescuer cycle. One may be in a victim mode, saying for example, "Poor me," then move into persecutor role saying, "It's your fault," then to the rescuer role of, "I'll help you," and then blaming the other person for getting them into that situation. Thus, even within one conversation a person can shift their position around the triangle. He can first accuse the other (persecutor), then blame others (victim), and then offer help (rescuer). It is the case that one person may move around the cycle, or various people may act out these roles in a static or moving fashion.

It is possible to get out of the victim role and the associated triangle by using the conflict resolution empowerment circle of the learner/leader/mediator (Cornelius & Faire, 2006). This is a far more positive shape and it gets you out of looking at things in a negative way. The learner/leader/mediator circle approaches situations as being challenging and as opportunities for growth and learning, rather than as negative experiences which are impossible to change. This is a way of empowering yourself and taking control of you.

What this means is that you might find it easier to look at a situation as being a learning experience rather than as, "I failed again." On one level there are no mistakes, just opportunities for learning. But the learning will come only when you see it as a situation to learn from. Otherwise, all you will see is a confirmation of how you are or how the world is. So, thinking in this manner will enable the changes to come.

PESSIMISTIC AND OPTIMISTIC THINKING STYLES

Seligman (1990) suggests that there are two main styles of habitual thinking that people engage in. These are pessimistic and optimistic styles.

These different ways of thinking may have an innate component and also come about due to our experiences in the world. While the basic stance may not be easy to change, it is possible for a pessimist to become more optimistic, and for a person who is overly optimistic to become more realistic. So, the questions to think about here are:

- What do I usually expect to happen?
- Do I worry a lot?
- Do I always or usually think/expect the worst?
- Do I often avoid doing things because I talk myself out of it?
- Do I often expect bad things to happen?
- Do I often expect the best, but fail due to a lack of effort?
- Do I usually blame myself when things go wrong?

- Or, when things go wrong, do I usually blame everyone else?

The aim with regards to thinking style is to become a little bit more realistic.

It is not the case that everything is always one's own fault, nor is it the case that it is everyone else's fault either. There are often multiple explanations for any particular event when things go wrong.

As discussed in chapter 2, if you accept responsibility for your part in the situation, then it is possible to find a way out of blaming and the role of being the victim. Victims as such are usually in a mindset of being pessimistic. And for a short time, this is okay, but to blame yourself totally for whatever occurred is unrealistic, usually.

In order to improve optimism, the explanation you give for a negative event should be based on an understanding that it is temporary rather than permanent, and specific rather than universal. You should also seek a reason for it happening due to circumstances or actions, rather than your own nature. For example, an explanation for doing not so well on a test for a pessimist would be, "I'm stupid," and, for an optimist, "I didn't do enough work for it."

The optimist has a better possibility of improving their level of effort and will be more likely to make the attempt, whereas the pessimist may just become depressed about being "stupid."

It is possible to be overly optimistic and not to pay attention to the reality of a situation. It is a good idea to do a reality check. What are other people saying about the situation? Are you disregarding aspects of reality? Questions to ask might be:

- Are my expectations unrealistic?
- Am I expecting others to fall into line or to obey my expectations?
- Am I thinking that I have total control over others and the situation, when I do not have this control at all?

People who are optimistic (but not overly optimistic) in thinking style tend to live longer, have a better quality of life, health and well-being. They may also be happier, and more able to cope with life than those who are pessimistic (Seligman, 1990). These are all good reasons to change your thinking habits, aren't they?

Optimists tend to cope better because they can bounce back faster after a setback and do not give up as easily as a pessimist. Pessimists tend to experience a greater amount of negative emotion including guilt and depression. They may also have lower self-worth and self-esteem.

If you use the techniques described in this book to address the goal of improving your optimism then, although it may take some time and effort, you will be rewarded by feelings of greater well-being. You will still have good days and bad days. Everyone does. The change will be that the low days will be a great deal higher than they are at present.

SUMMING UP

Through your beliefs about yourself, others and the world, you create your own reality. However, it is not that you can get to the bottom of your beliefs and suddenly know how you should think. This is because what can happen is that the beliefs, what you truly believe, might be hidden underneath in your unconscious. Or, at the very least, hidden under a great number of other beliefs and attitudes that you are more aware of on a day-to-day basis. In this event, you need to become a digger, an investigator into your own mind. The next chapter looks at ways of recognising your personal issues.

SUMMARY

- We all have core beliefs about how we see ourselves, others and the world.

- Core beliefs act as filters through which we perceive our world of experience.

- McKay and Fanning identify 10 core beliefs.

- It is good to be able to identify where you are at in relation to these core beliefs so that you are able to set goals for your personal growth and to improve them.

- Affirmations and counteractive statements are two tools to help you change your beliefs to being more positive.

- Investigating the past and finding evidence is a tool suggested by McKay and Fanning (1991) to help change your beliefs.

- The learner/teacher/mediator triangle is a more positive approach to life than the victim/persecutor/rescuer triangle.

- Optimism and pessimism are two styles of habitual thinking.

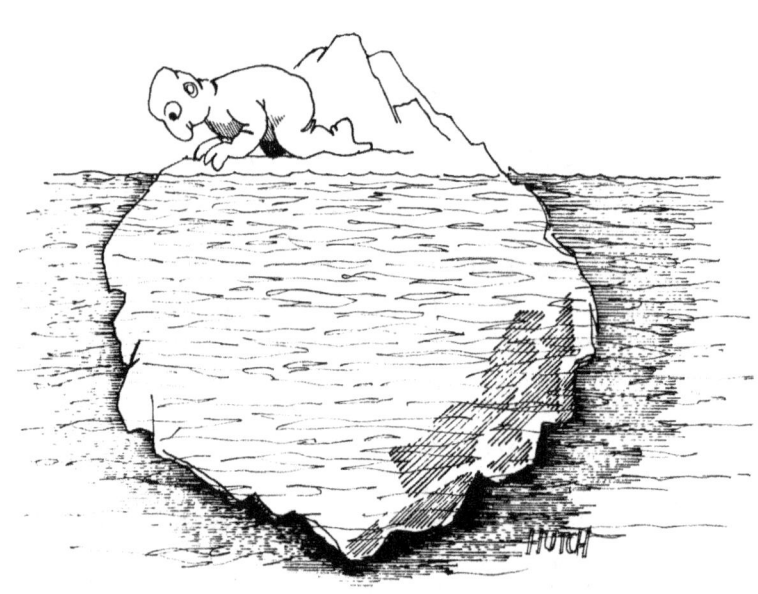

CHAPTER 6
DISCOVERING ISSUES

You may have already identified issues you want to work on in making changes in your life, but it is not always straightforward to discover these. This chapter shows how you can become more aware of issues that may be affecting your daily life, and details techniques to help you identify them. It also discusses metaphors and symbols as a way of both discovering and working on issues.

HIDDEN ISSUES

As discussed in chapter 1, the mind can be seen as an iceberg. Above the water are those things we are aware of. Underneath is all the rest—the 90% that we are not aware of. Some of the 90% will be parts of ourselves that, through upbringing or choice, we have forgotten or repressed. They haven't really disappeared—they have just been shoved down into the bottom part of the iceberg, otherwise known as the unconscious. This is often called disowning.

Important parts of our thinking that we have disowned may at times bubble to the surface in our behaviour. When this happens, we may deny their existence and thus continue disowning them. Such denial can operate on either a conscious or unconscious level. It occurs when we say to others, "No, I have no problem," when it is obvious to others that we do.

Denial can be a way of not admitting to ourselves that we have the choice to do anything about a problem. It is also a way of not taking responsibility for our behaviour. In other words, it is a way of staying within the victim role (see chapter 5).

Disowned parts of ourselves can also come to the surface when we see them in others. This is called projection. Again, this can operate as a form of denial because we can say, "That it isn't me, look it's the other person." This can be the case for both positive and negative attributes. For instance, a person who thinks that people of another culture or colour are inferior often feels inferior within themselves in some way. A positive example is admiring a person who speaks well and is assertive, when the admirer has the potential to do the same.

DISCOVERING THE SHADOW

The famous psychologist Jung called the disowned parts of ourselves the "shadow self" (Campbell, 1976). Becoming more aware of shadow issues helps us to take more control of our lives because it enables us to make conscious choices about what to do rather than allowing our unconscious to drive our behaviour.

How can you become more aware of the shadow issues that could be important to work on in your change process?

Strong reactions

One way is by identifying the behaviours of others that we have a very strong reaction to, both positive and negative. An interesting exercise to help you identify these things is to sit and think about, and write down, the characteristics or behaviours that you greatly admire in others, followed by those characteristics or behaviours in others that you cannot stand. In doing this, you are looking for things that prompt very strong or over-the-top reactions in you.

When you have made these two lists, have a think about how these might relate to personal issues you have. If you do not see any relation to your own issues straight away, just keep the lists in mind to think about.

Listening to what others say

Another way of discovering issues is to reflect on what others say to you about your behaviour and personality characteristics. What they say, especially if they know you fairly well, may well be accurate. Even if they are not always right, you may find that they are offering you something positive.

It is easier to look at responses and reactions when you are in a detached mode of self-monitoring, as discussed in chapter 3, so that you get the complete picture. The observations can then be compared to what others are saying. See what might be right for you.

For example, a few people may have said that you have a problem with alcohol or drugs. Look at whether you are spending more than 10% of your time in the pursuit of these, or you find that your finances are being compromised. Perhaps your relationships are going down the drain, or you are just not progressing in some areas. All of these can be an indication that something is not quite right. A further indication may be that while you were expecting progress, it seems as though you are actually going backwards. This suggests that you should reflect on why this might be happening. The reason may not always be what you think it is.

Self-honesty is important in this process of looking at your life. On the other hand, if someone tells you that you react too defensively to what they said, then that might be an indication that self-worth or another of the core beliefs could do with some improvement.

It is important to see that nothing that people do is without meaning. All you need to do is dig for the meaning. One particular behaviour may have a number of meanings attached to it.

In this process of self-reflection, look at the consequences your behaviour actually has for you in relation to how your life is going. Include in this any positive progress towards the goals you have set for yourself. Goal setting is looked at in greater detail in the next chapter.

Looking at patterns

Another way of discovering your issues is to look at patterns in your relationships. Take some time to consider patterns in a number of areas: for instance, close relationships, work and employment relationships (including those with co-workers and those in authority), or friendships.

Firstly, decide which relationships you are going to look at. Then write down the first incident you can remember, going into detail about how it started off, what was the next thing you noticed, what happened after that and so on, including how it ended or what the result was.

Do this process in the manner of a self-monitoring exercise. No judgement. Only what happened. However, do include the thoughts, feelings and behaviours that were involved. After you have done this, describe another one, until you have covered all of the incidents that you can remember, or have a list of the majority of them.

The next step is to think about the similarities between the incidents that you have written down. Do they follow the same pattern, or are there some differences? If there are differences in how they went, then ask yourself the question, "What made them different?"

Can you think up a phrase or short sentence to use as a theme? How does this naming a theme help you see what you are working on over this time? Are you still working on this?

If a particular subject, such as conflict, betrayal, or jealousy keeps on coming up a lot for you and you haven't considered that you need to work on this theme, then it might be a sign for you to start on this.

Looking at themes

Sometimes when you look back on your life, it may seem that there are one or two things that are hard for you: things that you seem always to have had trouble with in one form or another. This might be a life theme. And it might be that you will continue working on it (or them) all of your life. Some things are just harder than others to take in and get into your life. Others might be easy for you.

Divide the things that you do in your life into hard for you and easy for you. Those things that you find easy may well be skills that you can use to help you throughout your life. Those things you find hard will probably be things you need to work on in a conscious manner until they become part of your repertoire of behaviours. And even then, you may need to continue to work on them consciously, or in a planned format or routine.

ISSUES AND METAPHORS

Language is expressive and metaphorical. We say things are moving forward, standing still, not going anywhere, going backwards and so on. For this reason, the metaphors we use in everyday language can be helpful in discovering issues. For instance, if you feel that your life or situation is not going forwards, then you could try going for a walk and thinking about whatever problem or situation you are currently working on. Notice if any different possibilities arise as you are walking along. If you add to the process the conscious idea that you want to resolve the problem, and think consciously as you begin your walk that you are taking steps forward to work it through, then by the end of your walk you are likely to at least have gained greater clarity about the subject.

The use of imagery and metaphor in visual representation (as in drawing, painting, collages of pictures cut out from magazines) and in language, whether spoken or written, is also a powerful way of communicating to yourself and to others. If, for example you described how you were feeling as, "Like walking around in a thick fog," another person would understand this image and be able to picture it easily in their own mind. They would thus have a good idea of how you are feeling.

If you can find an image or metaphor to express how you are feeling, then this also makes it easier to work through and gain some clarity, either by yourself or with someone else. For example, using the thick fog metaphor, you could then ask yourself some questions and see if any answers occur to you:

- What would need to happen for the fog to lift?

- If there was no fog, what would be in front of me right now?

- Imagine being in the fog and doing something different, such as running or shining a torch—does anything different occur?

- What would happen if the sun shone more brightly and the fog disappeared?

When you have the answers to such questions, you will find some clarity to your situation and may well be able to make steps to move forward.

USING METAPHOR TO WORK ON ISSUES

The same idea of metaphor can be exemplified in a physical object.

If you have worked out the qualities that you want to improve on or to bring into your life more, find an object that represents those qualities or the essence of those qualities as a symbol of what you want to achieve.

The object can be quite small or even an everyday object that you already have. The important thing is to infuse that object with the things it now represents to you. Sometimes it is easier to get a new object rather than use one that currently has a lot of associations attached to it. However, see how it works to start off with if you have an object that you think will work for you.

In order to impress the object with what you now want it to represent for you, you could work out a little sentence that you can say to yourself or say out loud that states what the object is and what it now represents and embodies for you.

Place the object in a spot where you will see it every day to remind you of what you want to think about or focus on. Then, whenever you see it, its qualities, or what it represents or embodies for you, will come to your mind. It will thus be more likely that you will incorporate these qualities within you, or work on what the object embodies.

For example, a little plastic Buddha might represent or embody the meditation practice that you want to do. Placing your Buddha somewhere you'll see it every day would help to remind you both to do the meditations and to think more about how tense or stressed you feel.

Again, a small elephant might represent being strong in a situation, or a dolphin might represent movement or playfulness if you want to bring more fun in your life.

It is up to you to find the right object to represent those qualities or the focus you are attempting to gain.

SUMMARY

- In order to discover more about yourself, you need to pay attention to both your inner world and your outer world.

- To find the qualities that you have disowned, both positive and negative, think about those things you cannot stand or really admire in others.

- Look at patterns and themes in your life.

- The use of metaphor in everyday life can be helpful in finding clarity to move forward.

CHAPTER 7
SETTING GOALS

In order to make changes in your life, it is vital to set goals and to work towards them. This chapter discusses goal setting and working out how to go about achieving your goals of self-change.

WHY SET GOALS?

Goal setting is an important part of achieving what it is that you want in life. If you know what you want, then you can make the right choices towards achieving your goal and you will know when you have reached it. Setting goals helps to motivate you along the path you have chosen.

Some people seem to be able to set goals almost automatically. Others may have a vague goal that is not at all reality based. If you have a long-term goal to be happy, unless you have a concrete idea about what it is that makes you happy, you are not going to be able to make useful choices for yourself along the way towards that goal.

Effort and time are required to take the steps that will lead you to achieving your self-change goals. Unless you set the goals and work out strategies to go with them, nothing will happen. You need to take action to change.

WHAT ARE YOUR GOALS?

It is important to set realistic goals. Ensure that the goals you set relate to changing something that is possible to change. For instance, you may change from being a pessimist to being more optimistic, but it is unlikely that you will be able to become an optimist through and through. Keep your goals to the level of your behaviour and whatever is under your control, as discussed in chapters 1 to 3.

You want to change but what do you want to change? Look at all the areas of your life. These are: work/career; home/partner/children; extended family; friends/social life; health; leisure/hobbies; creativity/self-expression; and personal growth.

Once you have made a decision about what to work

on – for instance, becoming healthier - you need to break this broad aim down into achievable goals. The first step in thinking about how to do this is to set a goal that is SMART.

SETTING GOALS

Set a goal that is SMART:

Specific	Vague goals lead to half-hearted attempts to achieve them
Measurable	So that you can evaluate your progress
Attractive	So that you want to put in a sustained effort
Realistic	So that you are capable of achieving the goal
Time Framed	An appropriate time frame will enable you to work successfully towards your goal

If all these aspects are fulfilled, then it will be easier to work towards your goal, and to know when you have reached it.

Let's say that in order to become healthier you decide to lose weight and increase your fitness. You can set this goal up in the following framework:

Life Area   Physical health

Purpose   To be fit, to lose weight

Values   Respect for my body, physical health, achievement

You can add a project name to highlight the goal, for example:

Project Name   The Fit and Flexible Me

It can also help to think of a sign or symbol that stands for what you want to achieve. This doesn't have to mean anything except to you:

Sign/Symbol   Photo of myself when younger, looking active and fit

Now you can put this into the SMART framework:

Goal	Be fit and flexible, lose weight
Specific	Go to the gym for 1 hour, 3 times a week
Measurable	Keep monitoring log at home
Attractive	Will feel fit, flexible, more productive
Realistic	Gym close by, can go in evenings before dinner
Time Framed	Have weekly plan, start on Monday

As another example, let's say that in order to get more enjoyment out of your social life and relationships with friends you want to be more assertive:

Life Area	Social/friendships
Project Name	The Assertive Me
Sign/Symbol	A plastic bear
Purpose	To stand my ground

Values	Self-respect, personal growth
Goal	To be assertive in my daily life
Specific	To say, "No" to people when I don't want to do what they want me to do
Measurable	Will write all instances down in my journal every night
Attractive	Will be proud of myself, less hassled
Realistic	Will not take too much time
Time framed	Will do it daily when required

PROGRESS AND ACHIEVEMENT

Goals can be long-term, medium-term or short-term. If you have a long-term or medium-term goal, then you might need to work out the steps or strategies that you should put into action every week or fortnight in order to achieve it. These weekly or fortnightly goals allow you to check regularly how much progress you have made towards achieving the larger goal. Every time you see that you have achieved at least part of your planned actions, you need to give yourself a big pat on the back.

Goals need to be reviewed regularly. See what is working and what is not working. If something is working, then keep on doing it. If it's not working, then you need to do something different. Revisit your values and ensure that they are motivating you towards your goal. If you are not making progress, then maybe the goal needs to be changed, or perhaps the strategies and short-term goals need to be reviewed. If there is still no progress after a reasonable time, then maybe there is an issue that is blocking you and you might need some help.

Setting a maximum of three goals at any one time is more helpful to start with. It might be good to have at least one short-term goal along with long-term goals so that you can reach your short-term goal and tick it off the list.

The SMARTer your goals are, even long-term ones, the better. Thus, we could add a time frame to the fitness goal so that the goal becomes, "To be fit and flexible within 6 months."

WORKING ON QUALITATIVE GOALS

It is easy to work out goals when they consist of something that you can count and know for sure when you get there, such as saving up a certain amount of money.

It is not so easy to know when you have reached a goal like having a good relationship or being happy. How do you know it when you get there? And, when and if you do get there, what do you do?

Qualitative goals tend to be more dynamic and ongoing. Although it is possible to have an idea about what would be happening, or how you would be behaving with others, if you were happy, you need to keep on working on these kinds of goals. Your goal would probably include being happy on a continual basis, not just being happy for 10 minutes. Thus, you would need to keep on reviewing the things that made up your idea of being happy.

People tend to be happier when they feel they are doing something that is worthwhile in some way. What sort of meaning can you put on what you are doing in life? This can be having meaningful work or a meaningful life away from work. But whatever you do, in whatever part of your life, it would be nice to see it as meaningful. It is up to you to put the meaning onto it. And this will depend upon what is important to you. Perhaps have a look back now at your values and think about where you might be in relation to the core beliefs that were discussed.

CREATING SMALL GOALS WITHIN BIG GOALS

Example 1—'being happy'

Qualitative goals are easier to set and manage when you break them down into smaller components. If you have an overall goal of being happy, it is important to break this down into a number of supporting goals.

So, if you have a goal of being happy, what would that look like? How would you behave? How would others be? What is really involved in your being happy? It might actually entail other things like the values and beliefs that we have already looked at. So perhaps being happy is partly having peace of mind—what does that mean for you? How does that look? Perhaps being comfortable financially. Perhaps living a simple life. When you break the long-term goal down into smaller parts, it becomes easier to see what you are working on.

Break the goal of being happy down into its component parts and make these your long-term or medium-term goals, and then work out the strategies or steps to get you there. It is important to keep in mind that your goals need to have as their focus what you do—your actions. Each goal needs to be SMART.

Example 2—'a good relationship'

Let's say, for example, that you have a goal of a quality relationship. However, you have identified some past problems concerning communication in your relationship. What can you do?

Firstly, think about what a quality relationship would look like, both from the inside, i.e., from your perspective, and from the outside, i.e., as an observer looking at the relationship. When looking from the inside of the relationship, think about what you would be doing, saying, feeling, and how you would be responding and talking to/with your partner. Additionally, think about what would they look like, be saying and feeling in a quality relationship with you. Think about all of the aspects of your relationship.

The best thing to do in this is to communicate with your partner, so that you know where they stand in relation to how they see your relationship, and so your partner knows about your ideas on this. When in doubt, check it out verbally with them.

This goal will require a lot of thought, and perhaps reading, as well as talking. Relationships require negotiation. This takes a lot of communication and the idea of non-blaming is especially important in such communications, otherwise it might be difficult to move in a positive direction. The Conflict Resolution Network books are excellent for references on how to do this.

Once you have looked at your relationship and worked out what it is that you can do differently that might change the relationship, you can make this your goal. It might be something like treating your partner in a different way, saying things differently, being more assertive, or complimenting his/her behaviour. If you set this goal, monitor your relationship throughout the times you are together and write down in your journal the instances when the situation you are focussing on arises and what you try in response. You could also note the times when you put into practice your new behaviour, so that you can look back at a later date and see what happened. The more you practise your new behaviour, the easier it will become to use it regularly.

MOTIVATING YOURSELF

If you have set yourself a major goal and have worked out the supporting goals and steps, then decision-making is simplified. At any time that you need to make a decision, then you ask yourself the question, "What supports my goal?" If you make a decision to do something that does not support your goal, then do not do it. For example, if you have a major goal of buying a house, you may have to decide against expensive outings with friends. This doesn't mean that you don't go out, or don't spend money on an outing. The decision comes down to a choice between whether you want a house sooner rather than later.

ENSURING THAT YOUR GOALS ARE ACHIEVABLE

Ensure that your goals consist of very small steps that are achievable—e.g., 20 minutes' thinking time by yourself on your goals.

- Make a list of the steps that you need to take to achieve your goal. Be as concrete as possible.

- Work out what values are attached to each goal and why they are important (see chapter 4).

- Make a plan—priorities and steps.

- Review goals often—daily and weekly.

- If you find you are making progress, keep on doing what works (if it's not broken, don't fix it).

- If you are not making progress, review and plan a different way of doing the step. For example, you could add extra support (get a friend involved too), or change the step (if it isn't working, do something different).

- Often, circumstances intervene and affect your time frame. If this happens and it is out of your control, then change the time frame and go back to the step when you can.

- The goal might need to be changed. Consider this in the goal reviewing process.

SUMMARY

- Goal setting helps you to go forward in a direction you have chosen.

- Goal setting helps you make decisions more easily and motivates you generally.

- Goals need to be SMART: specific, measurable, attractive, realistic and time framed.

- Goals may consist of major goals (long-term), sub goals (medium-term) and minor goals (short-term action steps).

- All sub goals and minor goals support the major goal.

- If you have a qualitative goal, then you need to be clear about it so that you will know it when you reach it.

- All goals should be reviewed regularly.

- You need to be flexible at times. Sometimes circumstances change and you need to change goals, and revise them upwards or downwards.

CHAPTER 8
CONTINUING THE PROCESS— DEALING WITH NEGATIVE THOUGHTS AND EMOTIONS

One of the main things you may have to deal with in continuing the process of change is the impact of negative thoughts and emotions. These can get in the way of setting your goals and sabotage your intentions during the change process by pulling you back to old ways. This chapter provides some techniques that will help you continue your process when you get stuck, particularly as a result of negative thoughts and emotions, at whatever stage of your process they may arise.

MANAGING OLD AND NEW PATTERNS

When you start to change, you need to do things consciously until you learn the new behaviours and they become more automatic. However, you are likely to find that at this stage it is still very easy to slip back into old behaviour patterns. It is as though there is some inertia in old patterns. It can seem a lot easier not to change.

You may find that you give yourself all sorts of reasons as to why you shouldn't bother changing. This is the old behaviour patterns talking. Don't take any notice of them, or at least ignore them and continue on your path of determination to change.

It takes effort and energy to change. If you take a long-term view without beating yourself up over the occasional slip back, then you are more likely to achieve your goals. You need to be your own cheerleader and motivator. You and you alone can put this change into action. Be brave! Be courageous!

REPLACING NEGATIVE BEHAVIOUR WITH POSITIVE BEHAVIOUR

Some goals, such as to stop smoking, particularly lend themselves to self-sabotage. When you smoke, you fill time by smoking. When you find that you can stop, then what are you going to do instead? This could be an important aspect for you to consider.

If you are in this position, it is best to replace a negative behaviour with a more positive one. For instance, if you smoke to relax but are trying to give up smoking, instead of smoking, you could do some tensing and relaxing exercises. These may help you to get used to the idea that you can be easy and comfortable without smoking. Again, a bonus of stopping a negative behaviour is that you will have more energy and time to work on your positive goals. For example, instead of smoking you could go for a walk, which might also be meeting another goal. Considering what you can do instead and putting this into practice will also help in reducing any negative or worrying thoughts you may experience when you start changing.

STAYING IN CHARGE OF YOUR THOUGHTS

It is important to realise that you are not your thoughts. You can actually train your thoughts. You do not have to be at their mercy if you don't wish to be. Even if you are suddenly in the midst of an anxiety or panic attack, there is some control that you can gain. Of course, it is generally easier if you don't find yourself in the middle of an anxiety attack to begin with.

There are a number of ways that you can go about gaining more control over the things that appear to be controlling you. For instance, worrying is something that almost everyone does at some time. Some do it more often than others. The point is that worry is by definition not generally productive. In chapter 3, I discussed the importance of being in the present moment, in the now. If you are worrying about something you have already done, then you are going back to the past, and if you are worried about something that might happen, then you are putting yourself into the future—a future that is highly unlikely to occur. Usually, when a situation arises, ways of managing it and finding support will become available to you.

STOP SIGN TECHNIQUE TO CONTROL NEGATIVE THOUGHTS

This technique is particularly useful when you find you are having intrusive thoughts that appear to be somewhat obsessive (i.e., they just seem to keep popping into your mind without you really trying to think about them).

What you do once you are aware of these thoughts is to imagine a red and white stop sign in front of your eyes, and at the same time do a long-drawn-out silent scream of, "Stop" inside your head and body. It helps if you put all of your effort into this silent scream. Clenching your fists, and tightening the rest of your muscles may help, too. It is easier to do this lying down, and since these intrusive thoughts often come at night just before sleep or during the night, then it is easier to involve the whole body. When you do this, then the thoughts are obliterated for a time.

When you have done the stop sign once, after a short time you might notice that the intrusive thoughts are back again, so visualise the stop sign and do the silent scream again. You need to be persistent with this process. You might need to do it a few times before you find a real gap between the intrusive thoughts, but a gap there will be, and if you continue to be persistent then they should stay away long enough for you to get to sleep.

VISUALISING TECHNIQUES

There are quite a few good books around on the power of visualising. One of the reasons that it works is that it is a short cut to your brain. The brain does not recognise the difference between something that is real versus something that is imagined and believed to be real. The significance is in the experience. Your brain may not take notice of a single instance, but it might take more notice of something happening more often, or more regularly. You need to be persistent and keep on giving your brain the message so that it is noticed among all the rest of the clutter in your mind.

Images are the domain of the right side of the brain. This is the more visual/creative side of the brain, whereas the left side deals with more sequential things, such as logic, language and numbers. Since a picture speaks a thousand words, visualising can be very helpful as you work on your goals for change, especially in processing past events, practising future goals and gaining peace of mind within the present moment, as in meditative practice. Visualisation can also help directly with achieving certain goals, such as self-worth. However, if there are major issues impacting on your life, it is recommended that you do not attempt visualising without the help of a trained professional, at least in the first instance.

FIRE VISUALISATION FOR PROCESSING PAST EVENTS

Past events can be the events of the day or of the more distant past. You can use this fire visualisation for a daily letting go, or for dealing with the emotion of memories from some time ago. Once you get the idea of how visualisation works from the following examples, you will be able to use other images that may well be more appealing or appropriate to you than fire. For example, you could use a flowing river or a hot air balloon.

Daily letting go

Sit down at the end of the day and imagine that you are sitting in front of a small fire. The fire can be in a hearth or fireplace, or in the bush. Wherever it is, it is controlled and small. You are sitting in front of this little fire which is burning brightly, and you are watching the flames, and the burning wood, and staring into the orange, yellow and red flames. As you sit there, imagine that you can cast your mind back over the things that happened during the day, and pull out of yourself or take from your shoulders, all the negative emotions that you felt, all the negative self-talk that you said to yourself, and chuck them onto the fire. Watch those negative thoughts and emotions burn and go up in smoke up the chimney, or into the sky. Continue to throw thoughts and feelings that you do not want onto the fire for as long as you can sustain the images, but even a few minutes of concentration will be helpful, provided that you keep on doing it on a regular basis.

Reducing the emotion attached to memories of the past

Visualisation can also be used to reduce the amount of emotion that is attached to a memory of an event or experience you had. When you are doing this process by yourself, focus on events that you do not consider as traumatic—instead, think of one-off instances of being embarrassed, feeling guilty, resentful, jealous, or ashamed over an action or non-action, and so on. The point is that every time you think of the event, the negative emotion also comes up for you. What this means is that there is unfinished processing here and the ideal state would be to reduce the emotion to as close to zero as possible. You will not forget the memory, but when the emotion is to some extent detached from it, or completely gone, you are less likely to remember the event as often as previously. What this means is that you will be operating more in the present moment.

Find a time when you can be alone where you are not going to be interrupted or distracted for 5 to 10 minutes. You can even do this on a bus or train but please, not when you are driving. Imagine the small fire as described in the first visualisation. Think about the event/experience that you want to work on. Label the emotion. Get a range of how strong it is for you, between 1 and 10, with 10 being the strongest. This will give you an indication of where you are up to with processing the event.

When you have named the emotion and recorded how strongly you feel it, pull it out of wherever it is in your body—whether your guts, chest, or shoulders—and throw that emotion on to the fire. Watch it burn and go up in smoke, up the chimney or into the sky. Keep on throwing that emotion onto the fire for as long as you can manage at the one time. Five minutes is good, although even a few minutes of quality flame burning will work.

Every now and then you could find something else that needs to be thrown on the fire. For example, this could be another emotion that also went with the same experience, the thoughts that went with it, or, importantly, the belief it engendered in relation to you and the event's meaning. Continue to carry out this visualisation at least once a day over a period of two weeks. At this stage you should notice that the strength of the emotion that is attached to the event is nowhere near as strong as it used to be.

VISUALISATIONS TOWARDS THE FUTURE

Once you have processed some of the negative thoughts and emotions, then you are in a position to give yourself more positive input and build up your future by using visualisation.

Since the brain cannot tell the difference between reality and imagination, the more you practise an event in your mind, making it as real as you can, the better your brain will accept the practice as being real.

This process can therefore be used to calm yourself and help you to perform better before events that normally provoke anxiety in you. If you are involved in sports, this type of visualisation also enhances physical performance. Again, the main aim is to make the visualisation as real as possible, and not to miss even the fine details that might be there on the day. Repetition too will help. Some studies that have been done in the area of performance enhancement, especially in sports and training, suggest that visualisation of how you want to move also helps. For example, a swimmer may visualise having oil on the body to reduce water tension. People training with weights may visualise having heavier weights than they are actually training with. Visualising depends on the particular athlete but it is a common practice that works not only for elite athletes, but also for the normal person (see, for example, Lohr & Scogin, 1998).

If you work out all the details before you get into the visualisation, it will work more effectively when you actually do the visualising.

IMPROVING SELF-WORTH THROUGH VISUALISATION

If you have a goal of improving your self-worth, then you could imagine in great detail a scene that is in the future and where you are receiving a certificate (or similar) for achieving improved self-respect and self-confidence. Get all the details of who might be present and imagine this in as much detail as possible: the colours and sounds; what you would be thinking, feeling, and how you would be acting and behaving in that situation; what you would be saying and what would others be saying as well. Visualise this once a day for a couple of weeks and notice any differences at the end of this time. You might like to keep on using this visualisation for longer.

PRACTISING NEW BEHAVIOURS AND SITUATIONS

If you are working out ways to communicate better within the self-monitoring process, you can practise in your mind how you might think, feel, and behave before you actually do it in real life. The process of visualising and going through in your mind how it might be will certainly help you, and you are likely to feel more confident and prepared for the change of behaviour than you might otherwise be. For example, visualise yourself saying "No" if you are working on a goal of assertiveness. Imagine the situation in all its detail, including who is present and their positive reactions to your assertiveness.

DECLUTTERING YOUR MIND MEDITATION

It is possible to declutter your mind of unwanted thoughts and worries so as to create space for the thoughts that you want to focus on through meditation.

Meditation is not difficult but it does take effort and a bit of time to keep up the practice. The following is a basic approach.

To meditate, you do not need a secret chant or name. You can sit in a chair with your feet flat on the floor, or sit cross-legged on the floor with your back straight, depending on your choice. Make yourself comfortable—but not too comfortable—and close your eyes. The idea is not to go to sleep, but to stay aware of the now. Pay attention to your breath—as you breathe in, you can count in your mind 1, and then count 2 on the outward breath. Just notice how it feels as the breath goes in and out. In the present. In the now. Just be. Just breathe in on 1 and out on 2. That is the focus—the breath and the count. It doesn't matter if you find yourself thinking about what to do tomorrow. Just notice that this is what you are thinking and take yourself back to the focus of the meditation: the breath and counting 1 and 2. It is simple. You don't need to think. Just think 1 and 2 and remember to breathe. And whenever thoughts intrude, which they will, just notice them, and then take yourself back to the meditation. You don't need to upset yourself over how well or otherwise you are doing, because it does take practice. Just bring yourself gently back to the meditation when you notice that other thoughts intrude.

It is good to do meditation every day, and preferably for 10 minutes at a time.

STAYING ON COURSE

You can always get help in the form of an extra cheerleader to help you continue your process of change, but you are still the one who is required to put in the hours of monitoring, working out what it is that you want to do differently, putting plans into action, and working out what happened and whether anything did not go according to plan. A counsellor or life coach can be of benefit due to the fact that two heads are better than one and it is easier to work out what is really happening, including underlying unconscious motivations. However, it is still you who needs to do the real work, to begin to behave in ways that will help you to achieve the results that you want.

The main objective of the whole process is to realise that you are the only one who is able to make it all happen.

SUMMARY

- If you find yourself slipping backwards, see it as a test of your commitment to change.

- Negative thoughts and the stop sign technique.

- Use visualising techniques to help with both the daily letting go of negative thoughts and feelings, and as a way to process past emotional events.

- Visualisations to help improve future behaviour and performance.

- Regular meditation is also beneficial for mental clarity and focus.

CHAPTER 9
CONTINUING THE PROCESS— TROUBLESHOOTING

At times when you are trying to put your goals into practice, nothing seems to work. Often this means doing some more preparation and refining your goals. This chapter highlights some common problems and makes suggestions for overcoming them. It can seem like a lot of work, but you'll be far more likely to be successful in achieving your goals once you have cleared your path.

FRUSTRATION, ANGER AND REVENGE

Sometimes feelings such as resentment, the desire for revenge, and anger stop you from getting on with your goals. It is okay to feel these emotions. However, they are only hurting you, unless you are acting in ways that are illegal or non-respectful of others' rights.

If you just cannot get past an emotion connected with a situation, then one of the processes to let go of negative emotions described below could help. Pick the one that feels okay for you, or try them all and see which one works best:

- If you have identified an emotion and an event, then use the fire visualisation, or another that you are comfortable with, and throw away the negative emotions in this way (see chapter 8).

- Collect some drawing paper and crayons, pencils or oil pastels, and draw a revenge scenario happening to those who hurt you. Draw it only once. This is a letting go process not a hanging on process. See if the emotion changes after you have done this.

- Visualise yourself after you have let go of the emotions that are holding you back. How would you be looking? Feeling? Behaving? You may be very different in a positive way.

FORGIVENESS

Forgiving others and yourself is another important way to overcome emotions that are getting in the way of progress. A forgiveness ritual is one way of doing this. The following is an example:

Visualise that you are standing in front of the person you hurt or who hurt you. Now say the following to them (it seems to help if you vocalise the words, so whisper them at least):

"I ask your forgiveness, I forgive you, I forgive myself. I pray for your prospering, wherever you are. I bless you and release you to your highest good."

A forgiveness ritual can involve others, but it doesn't have to. See what happens when you carry it out by yourself and do not involve anyone else, except in your imagination. Forgiving yourself for being involved in this past experience can be a particularly important and difficult thing to do. Sometimes we are hardest on ourselves. After all, the forgiveness is really for you so that you can let the emotions go.

REDEFINING YOURSELF

It can be the case that being stuck in your change process is related to being stuck in a past experience. For instance, if you find that you are not willing to forgive yourself and others, even after you have done the letting go of resentment and other negative emotions, then you may be relying on that past situation to define who you are. When you do this, it is the same as being the victim (as discussed in chapter 5).

One way of moving on from this position is to identify yourself in another way. The new identification in no way changes what happened in the past, but it does change how you think about it now, in the present. So, in this instance it is more helpful to identify with a general characteristic rather than a specific one—for instance, as a survivor, rather than a survivor of sexual abuse. This more general label suggests the capacity to survive a lot of events and circumstances and so provides a strong and positive basis for future determination and direction.

To get an idea about how you define yourself at present, make a list of the things that you tell others about yourself. People often define themselves by their roles in society, whether they be work or family roles. Have a think about how you might be able to redefine yourself if you did not have these particular roles.

OTHERS' EXPECTATIONS

If you are stuck on your goals, it is worthwhile to ensure that the goals are yours and not based on others' expectations of you. Within society there are many expectations placed upon us to fulfil certain roles. It is up to you whether you actually take up these expectations or not. There is no written rule saying, for instance, that everyone has to have children. Just because your family talk about it does not mean that you should feel pressured. You can choose, although of course there are also personal circumstances that may intervene to deny the choice. Not everything is under our control.

The important thing here is to make the most positive choices you can, given the circumstances and other factors that may intrude. We can only do our best and learn along the way—that is all that we can expect of ourselves and of each other.

DIFFICULTIES IN CHANGING A HABIT

One way of overcoming problems in changing a habit or behaviour is to look at the belief that is underlying the habit (see chapter 5).

Another way is to look at the unconscious intention behind the behaviour. You can do this fairly easily by checking out the thoughts, feelings and body sensations that that take place when you imagine yourself doing the behaviour.

For example, if you are trying to give up smoking, you may discover that it is your way of relaxing. This unconscious intention is good, but the means whereby the relaxation is achieved is not. So, the idea would be to find a better way to relax and get rid of feelings such as anxiety, tension, or self-consciousness.

When you have identified whatever is going on behind a habit, it is likely to be easier for you to change it.

NOT ENOUGH CLARITY IN GOAL SETTING

If you can't get a handle on the goals you want to set, then you may get some clarity through engaging in a self-expressive medium.

Because creative and artistic methods work with metaphor (see chapter 6), they can enable breakthroughs in self-expression. They are also grounding. To put what is in our heads into a different medium, whether in clay, writing, music, painting, collage, or any other kind of self-expressive art, is changing the form of the original thought or feeling. The change of medium is what is grounding, and in the process the thought or feeling is turned to a concrete outer expression of oneself, rather than an inner abstract concept. Try it and see how the feeling is different from the inner to the outer.

- You could draw "Where I am right now," and on another sheet of paper "Where I want to be." Just allow the blank paper to draw itself if nothing comes to mind immediately. When you have finished, tell its story to yourself and see if any ideas occur to you from this.

- Draw your anger. Just hold the idea of your anger in your mind and again allow the page to say what it wants upon itself. This allows your unconscious to bring up and show you in a symbolic way what your anger might be.

- Draw your frustration and then, after you have finished, check within and see if this feeling is still as strong. Possibly, it is now lessened due to your noticing it and making it more objective and becoming more grounded.

Each person has his or her individual talents and skills in various areas. We don't have to work so hard at the things that come naturally to us as those that are not natural. If you have a talent in the medium you are using, then that is a bonus. However, you don't need to have a talent to engage in creative self-expression.

INABILITY TO SET MEANINGFUL GOALS

If the goals that you come up with don't have much meaning for you and you find them unattractive and unchallenging, then it may be helpful to look further at yourself and your world view.

Some people have a feeling that something is missing in themselves, a feeling of being empty. This feeling could be because you are not expressing some aspect of yourself, perhaps an ambition or interest that you have not been able to fulfil. It could also be because your beliefs about yourself and the world need to include some extra dimension concerning purpose, or spirituality. In both of these, the missing element is about the need for meaning in some area of life.

In thinking about meaning, it is important to note that you create the meaning of your 'being in the world'. To find answers for yourself, you first have to ask some questions. For example, asking, "Why am I here?" may be helpful for some people, but it might be more productive to ask, "What can I do now that I am here?" (Since we really didn't have a choice about getting here in the first instance). Another question might be, "Given who I am right now, what can I do about making my life better?" As discussed in chapter 7, be specific and analytical about the things that you want to change.

CHECKING PROGRESS

If the same thing keeps on happening, despite your attempts consciously to change it, you could ask yourself the question, "Is it happening exactly the same way, or is there some slight progress forwards?" (i.e., some more positive elements about the situation than last time).

- Look at what is the same and make a list, then rate them in relation to their importance in every other situation. Where is the pattern?

- Look at what is different. Is what is different something that you have worked on recently? If yes, then give yourself a pat on the back for making some progress.

- What do others say about the situation or pattern? Are they right?

- Are you working on the wrong aspect of the problem?

- If nothing new comes out of this analysis, then look on it as a test or challenge and keep on plugging away at changing your values, beliefs, and the process of change.

- Review your goals—maybe the goals need to be changed or the steps towards them need to be changed.

- If you had a purpose in life, what would it be? It might be to face up to and learn to overcome the things that you find most difficult.

From the list below, think about those which are the most difficult for you in both a general and a specific sense. You might like to make one of these into a personal growth goal:

- fear, the unknown, dealing with unexpected situations

- leading, being independent, taking action, listening to yourself

- nurturing oneself or others, supporting oneself or others

- self-expression, creativity, communication with others, having fun

- planning, attending to details, working hard, dealing with frustration

- flexibility, dealing with change, being too scattered

- responsibility, balance in one's life, harmony, artistic beauty

- getting a balance between having one's own space and being with others, self-critical, understanding how things work, spirituality

- authority, business, managing oneself and others

- finishing things off, getting the big picture, selfishness, arrogance

GETTING HELP

If you have attempted to use this book and put into practice your self-change goals, but you have not made any progress over some time, then it would be a good idea to get some help in the form of a counsellor or life coach.

SUMMARY

- When you are stuck in the process of change, there are things you can do to become unstuck.

- Look at the underlying belief or unconscious intention behind a habit to make it easier to change.

- Look at patterns and see if there is progress in any way, because you might be missing something that is different which does indicate progress.

- Self-expression and creativity, especially in the form of drawing and writing, are helpful to becoming unstuck as they are grounding and objectify what was inner to outer.

- Questions about meaning and purpose can be helpful in redefining who you are and how you want to change.

- If you are still feeling stuck, then an appropriate professional may be of help.

CONCLUSION

Now that you are at the end of the book, I hope you have discovered at least one thing to work on for change.

Once you have decided to change an aspect of your life and have taken responsibility for it, develop a self-monitoring goal and keep a journal for at least a short time to see what is actually happening right now as far as that aspect of your life is concerned. Do your research into whatever aspect of behaviour you wish to change and, having read chapter 7 on goal setting, work out your goal of self-change.

Working out the values that are important to you will help you set your goals. You have worked out which core beliefs you want to be higher on and maybe want to set a goal around these. Perhaps you have looked at your issues and want a goal around them too. Go for a maximum of 3 goals at a time. Don't forget that if you are learning a new behaviour or way of doing things, then it may take about a month before it becomes an automatic response, and before that time is up you need to think consciously about carrying out that behaviour.

Give yourself time to change. It doesn't happen overnight. However, if you keep on taking small steps in the present towards your goal then you will reach it. The SMARTer your goals are, the better. When you have achieved your goals, give yourself a big pat on the back. You will be able to look back on the process of change and see how far you have come. So, all the best in your future, may your life become the best it can be, and may you reach your potential.

Diana Hutchison

REFERENCES

Aisbett, B. (1996) Letting IT Go. Harper Collins: Australia

Berne, E. (1964) Games People Play. Penguin: USA

Bolton, R. (1986) People Skills. Prentice Hall: Australia

Bourne E.J. (1995) The Anxiety & Phobia Workbook. New Harbinger: USA

Branden, N. (1985) The Art of Self-discovery: A Powerful Technique for Building Self-esteem. Bantam: New York

Burns, D.D. (1999) The Feeling Good Handbook. (Revised ed.) Plume: New York

Capacchione, L. (1979) The Creative Journal: The Art of Finding Yourself. Newcastle Publishing Inc: California

Cornelius, H. & Faire, S. (2006) Everyone Can Win: Responding to Conflict Constructively. (2nd ed.) Simon & Schuster: Sydney

Davis M., Eshelman E.R. & McKay M. (1995) The Relaxation and Stress Reduction Workbook. (4th Edition) New Harbinger: USA

Dowrick, S. (1997) Forgiveness and Other Acts of Love. Penguin: Australia

Dowrick, S. (2000) The Universal Heart. Penguin: Australia

Dyer, W.W. (1995) Your Sacred Self. Harper Collins: New York

Edwards, Gill (1993) Stepping Into the Magic: A New Approach to Everyday Life. Piatkus: London

Ferrier, L. & Briese, M.D. (1992) Dance of the Selves: Uniting the Male and Female Within. Fireside: New York

Gawain, S. (1978) Creative Visualisation. Whatever Publishing Inc: California

Gawain, S. (1986) Living in the Light. Whatever Publishing Inc: California

Gawain, S. (1993) The Path of Transformation. Nataraj Publishing: California

Gendlin, E.T. (1978) Focusing. Bantam Books: New York

Graham, H. (1992) The Magic Shop. An Imaginative Guide to Self Healing. Rider: London

Graham, H. (1995) A Picture of Health. How to Use Guided Imagery for Self-healing and Personal Growth. Piatkus Publishing: London

Grant, A.M. & Greene, J. (2001) Coach Yourself. Pearson Education.: London

Hanna, P. (1998) Believe and Achieve! Penguin: Australia

Hillman, J. (1996) The Soul's Code: In Search of Character and Calling. Random House: Australia

Hay, L.L. (1984) You Can Heal Your Life. Specialist Publications: Australia

Jung, C.G. (1971) The Portable Jung. Campbell, J.(ed.) Penguin Books: USA

King, Petrea (1988) Quest for Life. Equinox: Sydney

Landsberg, M. (1997) The Tao of Coaching. Harper Collins: London

Lohr, B.A. & Scogin, F. (1998) 'Effects of Self-Administered Visuo-Motor Behavioral Rehearsal on Sport Performance of Collegiate Athletes.' Journal of Sport Behavior 21, (2), 206-218

Matthews, A. (1988) Being Happy! Media Masters: Singapore

Matthews, A. (1997) Follow Your Heart: Finding Purpose in Your Life and Work. Seashell Publishers: Australia

McKay, M. & Fanning, P. (1991) Prisoners of Belief. New Harbinger: USA

McKay, M. & Fanning, P. (1992) Self Esteem. New Harbinger: USA

Mindell, A. (1990) Working on Yourself Alone: Inner Dreambody Work. Arkana: UK

Norwood, R. (1994) Why Me Why This Why Now: A Guide to Answering Life's Tough Questions. Century: London

Pearsall, P. (1999) The Heart's Code. Bantam: Australia

Proto, L. (1989) Who's Pulling Your Strings? Thorsons Publishing Group: UK

Rokeach, M. (1968) 'A Theory of Organization and Change Within Value-Attitude Systems.' Journal of Social Issues 24 (1), 13-33

Rowe, D. (1995) Dorothy Rowe's Guide to Life. Harper Collins: London

Samways, L. (1997) The 12 Secrets of Health and Happiness. Penguin Books: Australia

Seligman, M.E.P. (1990) Learned Optimism. Random House: Australia

Seligman, M.E.P. (1993) What You Can Change... And What You Can't. Fawcett Columbine: New York

Spencer, R. & Rossmanith, A. (1995) Stop Struggling: The How to of Personal Change. Harper Collins: Australia

Stone, H. & Winkleman, S. (1989) Embracing Ourselves: The Voice Dialogue Manual. New World Library: California

ABOUT THE AUTHOR

Diana Hutchison is an author, counsellor and coach whose life-long passion for self-development has led her to create a series of books in the self-help genre. Being drawn towards understanding multiple ways and modalities, she sought to create meaning for herself and her life which has meant that her unique holistic approach explores all levels of being: physical, mental, emotional and spiritual, leading to a perspective of self-healing which enables the best results for her clients. This multiple perspective has inspired the authorship of the Practical Guide series, of which this book is the first.

COMING SOON

Second book in this series:
A Practical Guide for Young Adults

Third book:
A Practical Guide for Grief and Loss

To learn more about what Diana offers for your self-healing and to be updated on her upcoming books, please visit www.dianahutchison.com and sign up for her newsletter.

www.dianahutchison.com

www.ingramcontent.com/pod-product-compliance
Lightning Source LLC
Chambersburg PA
CBHW070257010526
44107CB00056B/2490